HOW TO EMBALM YOUR

MOTHER-IN-LAW

OR

ALL YOU EVER WANTED TO KNOW ABOUT
WHAT HAPPENS BETWEEN YOUR LAST BREATH
AND THE FIRST SPADEFUL

BY

ROBERT T. HATCH

A CITADEL PRESS BOOK
Published by Carol Publishing Group

First Carol Publishing Group Edition 1993

A Citadel Press Book
Published by Carol Publishing Group
Citadel Press is a registered trademark of Carol Communications, Inc.
Editorial Offices: 600 Madison Avenue, New York, N.Y. 10022
Sales and Distribution Offices: 120 Enterprise Avenue, Secaucus, N.J. 07094
In Canada: Canadian Manda Group, P.O. Box 920, Station U, Toronto,
    Ontario M8Z 5P9
Queries regarding rights and permissions should be addressed to Carol Publishing Group, 600 Madison Avenue, New York, N.Y. 10022

Carol Publishing Group books are available at special discounts for bulk purchases, for sales promotions, fund raising, or educational purposes. Special editions can be created to specifications. For details, contact Special Sales Department, Carol Publishing Group, 120 Enterprise Avenue, Secaucus, N.J. 07090

Library of Congress Catalog Card Number 81-83087

ISBN 0-8065-1420-5

Manufactured in the United States of America

10 9 8 7 6 5 4 3 2 1

TABLE OF CONTENTS

PROLOGUE

ACKNOWLEDGMENTS

PROLOGUE

The prologue to this story is LIFE. Grab it with all the gusto possible! Don't waste a precious moment of it. Love and be loved in return; show kindness to all; use the powers God gave you; and above all, be grateful to Him for putting you on this earth and allowing you immortality through the use of these wonderful gifts!

For once we complete life's passage, we enter a realm where two divergent forces control our destiny; the undertaker our body, and God our soul.

There are no tickets required on this, the inescapable and final voyage. Once the platform between life and death is crossed, there is no turning back. A series of events alter the journey slightly for each individual, but the destination is always the same--THANATOS.

To explain this journey may require some indelicacy. It is necessary, however, if we are to explore the burial process. Certain descriptions, although distasteful, are factual. Our body, in order to reach its resting place, may go through some unpleasant stages.

We have all gone through many unpleasant stages during life. From the first embarrassment of vomiting with another looking on, to the sight of torn and bleeding bodies at an accident scene, our demeanor accustoms itself to the realities of life.

Why then can we not prepare ourselves for the realities of death?

That is the intent of this book.

ACKNOWLEDGMENTS

My thanks to the following people without whose contributions this book would not be possible: John C. Florin, Virginia Stuck, Vance Ferguson, Dr. Gerald N. Beal, Dr. Samuele Bacchiocchi and my dear mother-in-law whose candies and pies sustained my sweet tooth and whose lovely daughter nourished my other needs.

R. T. H.

1

HOW TO BE IMMORTAL

CROSSING THE BORDER

Senescence begins
And middle age ends
The day your descendants
Outnumber your friends.

Ogden Nash

1

The desire for immortality is as old as man himself. It is woven throughout the history of the Egyptians, Greeks, Hebrews, Aborigines and every early society.

Philosophers have espoused theories, scientists have demonstrated its inapplicability, leaving the cudgel to be picked up by the theologians.

Their discussions are theoretical and too extensive to be covered here.

How then can we become immortal?

Many believe their immortality will only be achieved through the remembrances of their children and friends. It is well and good if our deeds of love live after us. But it is ill-gained immortality if the words of Shakespeare are true: "The evil that men do lives after them, the good is oft interred with their bones."

Certainly a form of immortality is achieved through remembrances from generation to generation. Our children quote our thoughts and sayings to our grandchildren; but alas, soon these are forgotten and immortality ceases!

Is this then the immortality we seek--or is it this, to live to an old age, perhaps 300 years or so?

NEW IDEAS IN SCIENCE

Scientists have wondered why man has to die. The trillions of cells that make up his body should be able to divide indefinitely. In tests being conducted it has been demonstrated that the human cell tends to divide approximately fifty times. It is believed that each cell has its own "death clock." The factors that affect this clock may be internal or external. Several theories have been promulgated to explain the aging in the cells.

Experiments have shown that cells taken from a new born will double about 50 times before they cease to function.

Likewise, cells taken from a middle-aged person will multiply about 25 more times. A few more times of multiplying are all that is left in elderly cells.

Some scientists believe this clock to be in the nucleus of the cells. Through research, conducted by such eminent authorities on aging as Dr. George Sacher of the Argonne National Laboratory and Dr. Leonard Hayflick of California's Children Hospital Medical Center in Oakland, much information of cell division has been collected.

If the nucleus of an aged cell is replaced by a young nucleus, the cell continues to multiply to its predetermined number.

Likewise, if an aged nucleus is transferred to a young cell, the cell ceases to multiply after a total of approximately 50 doublings has occurred.

The death clock in a cell is turned off when the cell is frozen. Amazingly though, the count is continued from where it left off, when the cell is thawed out—and runs out around the 50 doublings mark! The cell has a memory that transcends "death" by freezing.

Ironically, immortality is within the reach of each and every cell, but only through an injection of malignant causing virus. Cancer cells properly fed will continue to live on indefinitely.

Among the theories espoused, one that is gaining considerable support is Dr. Sacher's "good gene" hypothesis. This states that among the countless complex chemical reactions taking place constantly, that mistakes are certain to happen. Some mutations appear among the trillions of genes at work. This may occur from internal, accidental or environmental sources such as radiation or viruses.

The "good genes" repair the mutations and prevent the body from aging rapidly. This has found support from studies by Ronald Hart and Richard Setlow on seven mammals.

They found that cells damaged by exposure to ultraviolet radiation were able to repair the genetic mishaps. The DNA (deoxyribonucleic acid) repair rate occurred much greater in the long-lived animals than the short-lived species. This suggests that nature is ensuring the species survival by allowing the parents to be around long enough for the DNA repair mechanism to function.

Another theory states that the aging process is built into the genetic code which shuts down the cells at a pre-determined time. Thus time allows for the procreation of the species and off-spring rearing period; after this the parent is no longer needed.

A third theory proposes that errors occur and slowly build up in the genes. Eventually they interfere with the functions of the cell.

Another theory, called "running out," suggests that the cell contains a number of genes, most of which are not turned on. A non-working gene replaces a malfunctioned one until the cell eventually runs out.

A theory proposed by this author is that each individual creates within himself a chemical reaction which speeds up or slows down the cells multiplying capability. Thus a hyperactive individual may speed up the multiplying process and literally burn himself out. A slow moving phlegmatic person, the kind whom nothing seems to bother, produces a chemical change which retards the cells multiplication and allows an 85 to 95 year life span.

The author is basing his theory on observation alone. He has met many people who are completely unruffled by life and its exigencies. Consistently, when checking their geneaology, they have come from parents who lived to a ripe old age.

The young "do-ers" who are millionaires by age 30 often have shortened life spans on the whole. In many cases their parents likewise died early and didn't live to see the success of their offspring.

Immortality then may come through many additional years being added to our lives. It may come from the memories our loved ones carry of us. It may come from the survival of the spirit.

Probably the most positive (and expensive) way is to build a gigantic, indestructible tomb to yourself. Even after thousands of years, we know the name of the great Egyptian King Cheops whose remarkable pyramid survives through the ages. This is immortality!

2

THE ANSWER TO LIFE

THEOLOGICAL

*Said Descartes, "I extoll
Myself because I have a soul
And beasts do not." (Of course
He had to put Descartes before the horse.)*

Clifton Fadiman

2

Philosophers for centuries have groped for the answer to the question "What is life all about?" Religious leaders have tried their hand at interpreting the Bible in order to answer this most complex and evasive question.

Hundreds of books have been written, thousands of opinions have been given and still no one knows the truth. It seems it was not meant for this answer to be given to us while we are still alive.

About 35 years ago this answer was given to my sister and me in what was an extraordinary way. It had such an impact that I remember it today as if it had occurred last week.

We were in our early twenties. She was married, and being proud of her new home, would occasionally ask me over for an evening while her husband worked nights.

One evening we were sitting around talking and having a cup of coffee. Our conversation varied from current events to personal acquaintances to religion.

Of the four children in our family, she and I were particularly close. We were only 20 months apart and so spent much of our childhood playing together--sharing many tribulations, enjoying many successes. We couldn't have been more close if we were fraternal twins.

I preface our experience with these remarks to explain how closely we thought. Perhaps this may have accounted for the miraculous way we were able to reach and maintain a level of awareness not akin to normal rationalization.

This one particular summer evening apparently both of us were in a relaxed mood. A mood in which thoughts could freely flow and the interchange be understood by each without deep explanations.

Our topic being religion was normally shallow as neither of us were students of the subject--nor did our background add much depth to it. We were raised in a home where after the Sunday school years, church was attended mainly on Easter and Christmas Eve. And that was about all.

As I recall there was nothing that sparked our conversation on the meaning of life. We were just searching for answers like everyone else.

She would mention a happening in the Bible that she remembered from her childhood. Then I would say what I remembered about it.

This kind of conversation continued, but gradually got deeper. What she would say needed no explanation to me--I just understood it. And this was happening with her. We soon reached a stage where we were in total agreement and we didn't know about what.

As we progressed beyond this stage, we would alternately state truths about life. Where they came from or how we knew them, neither of us can remember. But the most amazing things were coming out of our mouths as we built step by step to the final answer to life.

And we reached the pinnacle and there before us was the total and complete raison d'etre--our reason for being alive. The answer was given to us and we knew that if we knew it our lives were ended. In other words, only the dead are privy to this information--and yet we had it and were still alive.

Suddenly we both broke out in a chill. We literally shook from fright--or whatever emotion we were feeling at that time. Our teeth chattered and we shivered uncontrollably for several minutes. How long this lasted I'm not sure, but when we finally stopped, we sat exhausted staring at each other. Afraid to speak. We both knew, without speaking that we had experienced a total understanding of life.

When we were once more composed she said, "Let's have another cup of coffee." As she got up, she said, "Come into the kitchen with me. I'm scared." She didn't have to ask as I didn't want to be left alone either. I followed her into the kitchen but neither of us spoke for several more minutes.

After we were once more seated in the living room, I said, "Betty, what happened?"

She said, "I don't know. I just know that we experienced a happening that no one will ever believe."

As we sat there recovering we agreed to try and retrace our steps to arrive at our mutually-reached deduction.

The steps were tedious to retrace. The statements and reasoning came much harder the second time. Our mind would draw a blank on how we went up the various levels of reasoning. We would catch a thought or phrase here but then lose the next logical step.

As we groped our way up, the explanations needed help and neither of us could give it.

We went as far as we could toward the final solution, but it failed us! The answer was not to be given to us again. And we knew why. We were still alive!

The step by step reasoning took us on the following course: God is the Father, the Son and the Holy Ghost. Likewise man is a triumvirate. He is body, mind and soul.

The body and mind cease to have any function at death, but the soul lives on. God is made of all the souls and each goes back to the **master** soul. It becomes a part of it. When a new babe is born, part of the soul is broken away for the babe to use.

This new soul may have talents from previous usage; may have remembrances from previous existences. The baby grows and adds its talents and abilities to the soul. When it dies, the master soul grows by these qualities. In other words, God grows, giving him the total understanding of us all. That is why he knows our prayers. We are part of him and he is all of us!

This gave us the answer as to why prodigies are so talented at such a young age. It may explain the deja-vu we experience when we feel we have been to a place before. Or had an experience before. Yet we know we have never been there previously. It may explain many phenomena not understood in earthly reasonings.

Regardless of what else this experience has done for us, it has made us aware that there **is** a reason for our life and that we will most certainly find it in the hereafter.

3

LIFE AFTER DEATH

OLD DR. VALENTINE
TO HIS SON

Your hopeless patients will live,
Your healthy patients will die.
I have only this word to give:
Wonder, and find out why.

Ogden Nash

Certainly a book about death would not be complete without a discussion of "life-after-death" experiences. There has been considerable material written recently regarding these unique happenings. Apparently however, these occurrences have been recorded for over 175 years!

In 1806 these was an article published in the **Evangelical Intelligencer** relating the experiences of Reverend William Tennent. This story, anonymously written at the time by Elias Boudinot, LL.D, was incorrectly credited to a Reverend Dr. Alexander.

Reverend Tennent, for three days was to all outward appearances, dead. His physician refused to believe the signs and resolutely attempted to revive him.

On the third day success was achieved. Upon awakening from his death-like trance, he was unable to remember anything that happened during his coma.

With the help of his family and friends, he gradually recovered his memory and related the extraordinary experience that follows: "While I was conversing with my brother on the state of my soul, and the fears I had entertained for my future welfare, I found myself, in an instant, in another state of existence, under the direction of a superior Being, who ordered me to follow him. I was accordingly wafted along, I know not how, till I beheld at a distance an ineffable glory, the impression of which on my mind it is impossible to communicate to mortal man. I immediately reflected on my happy change, and thought--'Well, blessed be God! I am safe at last, notwithstanding all my fear.' I saw an innumerable host of happy beings, surrounding the ineffable glory, in acts of adoration and joyous worship; but I did not see any bodily shape or representation in the glorious appearance. I heard things unutterable. I heard their songs and hallelujahs of thanksgiving and praise, with unspeakable rapture. I felt joy unutterable and full of glory. I then applied to my conductor, and requested leave to join the happy throng: on which he tapped me on the shoulder and said--'You must return to the earth.' This seemed like a sword through my heart. In an instant, I recollect to have seen my brother standing before me, disputing with the doctor. The three days during which I had appeared lifeless, seemed to me to be not more than ten or twenty minutes. The idea of returning to this world of sorrow and trouble gave me such a shock that I fainted repeatedly. Such was the effect on my mind of what I had seen and heard, that if it be possible for a human being to live entirely above the world and the things of it, I was that person. The ravishing sounds of the songs and hallelujahs that I had heard, and the very words that were uttered, were not out of my ears, when awake, for at least three years."

A most amazing experience, graphically described and not unlike many hundreds of others that have been recorded. In doing further research for this chapter, the author personally interviewed a number of people who have had similar experiences. An interesting fact was discovered that wove itself into their story in each case. This was a power that each possessed after they had "come back" from the beyond.

To illustrate a couple of examples:

Leo G., huskily-built, had a severe hernia attack while stationed in Germany in 1951. He was given a spinal injection to numb the lower part of his body for an operation. Apparently he was allergic to the spinal, or else his childhood fear of anything penetrating his spine, caused his body to go into massive convulsions.

His heart stopped and he "died" on the operating table.

He remembers his body separating with part of it floating above and the remaining part on the table. He could look down and watch the doctors and nurses frantically trying to revive him.

He remembers floating away and finding himself in a long tunnel. Travelling through the tunnel in slow motion, he proceeded toward a light at the end. Emerging from the tunnel he found himself among a number of white-robed figures communicating with him mentally. Although he does not remember what was expressed silently, he does remember feeling an aura of complete peace surrounding him.

The marvelous weightless feeling must be akin to what the astronauts feel in space. He wanted to stay there and enjoy the complete freedom from worry and tension, but it was not to be.

He suddenly found himself back in the tunnel and without experiencing movement through it, he found himself back in the hospital operating room. The doctors had successfully revived him.

As a result of this experience, Leo is a changed man--spiritually, mentally and physically. His body chemistry has changed to such a marked degree that he is unable to take medicine of any kind. The simplest tablet, such as Valium, will knock him out for a day or two.

Leo feels that there is something that he was put on earth to do. He does not know what it is, but knows it will be accomplished before he dies--which will be on January First.

Leo is able to predict disastrous events concerning members of his family. These predictions come to him at night while in a semi-awakened state. They are as vivid and real as any day-time experience.

In one such state, he saw his father and future wife's brother (whom he hadn't met) sitting at a large desk. On the desk was a calendar showing clearly the date of his death--January One. He and his wife never leave the house on that date and are sure that will be his last day alive. One might think he has programmed his death if it were not for the other strange visions he has had.

At one point, he saw his son with his chest covered with blood. Within a five month period, his son came down with a strep throat. Because of its seriousness it led to heart failure. He was rushed to the University of Michigan Hospital and had open heart surgery. The boy was only five years old! He is now sixteen and doing well.

Leo awakend one night at 1:13 a.m. He told his wife that his mother and father had been in an accident. Later when the facts came out, they did indeed have an accident and the police report recorded the time as 1:13 a.m.!

Many other prognostications have come true. In fact whenever an out-of-town relative calls, the first thing they ask is "Leo, did you dream about ME?"

Leo never had this power before his out-of-body experience and relates it directly to that event.

A similar "gift" was given to Len K. after his recovering from a three-day coma during which he was given up for dead.

In the fourth grade young Ken came home from school one day. He was playing with a cat when it scratched him. He didn't think much of it until he became deathly ill. His condition, called "cat fever" in those days, can lead to encephalitis. He slipped into a coma from which he could not be aroused.

During this period he found himself alone on a huge desert. Just as suddenly he was transported upward at an alarming speed. Although he could see no walls he felt as if he were in a tube moving upward toward a blue area.

As he got closer a bright light surrounded him. He heard two voices off to one side. One said, "We've got someone else here." He was asked then "Why are you here?" He answered that he didn't know. They asked his name. Something about their voices allayed all fears of his and he felt as if he had complete communication with them. He felt as if his whole life flashed before him--every word, every deed he had ever done.

At first he wanted to go back to his room but they told him to wait. They had to check something out and then he could go back.

He knew he was in a room, but there were no walls or doors. His acquaintances went through a door that he couldn't see. He started crying and one came back saying "Don't be afraid."

The other came back and said he wasn't supposed to be there. That there was something he was supposed to do in life before he could come back.

They took him into another room which was brighter than any he had ever seen before. They told him he would feel the light going through him and he would be cured. He felt the warmth from the light completely encompassing him.

After this light treatment he wanted to go through another door with them but they refused. They said on the other side was the most beautiful place he would ever see. Everything was colorful and peaceful and that anything he ever imagined was there.

He asked if his uncle were there and they nodded yes. Would his pet dog be there some day? Again a nod. They said he knew everybody there and they knew him.

He said he didn't want to leave but they said it was time to go. Suddenly he found himself descending rapidly. As he looked down, he saw the trees surrounding his home. Then the roof of his home and finally his room with himself on the bed. He saw his dog leave the bed and go downstairs. When his mother saw the dog, she immediately went to his room. Tearfully she welcomed him back. Six weeks later he was up and playing as strong as ever.

Countless times since then he has experienced pre-cognition. He has told his wife prior to a happening what was to occur. The events inevitably deal with disaster and death.

There was the time that he felt a death was to occur in a certain neighborhood. He could not pinpoint which of two homes would be the scene of the event, but he knew it was going to happen. Shortly before morning his brother-in-law, who was on the Sheriff's Department, was called to investigate his first suicide. A neighbor had killed himself with a shotgun. He lived in one of the two homes Len had pre-determined as being the fatal site!

There was the time he passed a local marina and saw three children walking. He felt something was going to happen to the owner and pictured him lying on the ground in a certain position dressed in a white shirt and black slacks.

Two days later, the owner fell from a ladder while working on his sign. He died instantly of a broken neck and was in the position described by Len K. to his wife previously. He was dressed in a white shirt and black slacks!

At one point he felt himself walking through a large field with scores of dead people lying about. He felt helpless. What could he do with this knowledge? Shortly after, it came out in the papers that there was a tremendous propane explosion that killed many. The picture in the paper was a duplicate of his vision.

He feels helpless in having this knowledge and not being able to warn people in advance. But what can he do?

To fulfill what he believes is his purpose on earth, he became a medic. With his specialized knowledge he has helped dozens of people to have their second chance—just as he had his.

4

BIOLOGICAL TRANSITION

AN EPITAPH

A lovely young lady I mourn in my rhymes:
She was pleasant, good natured, and civil sometimes.
Her figure was good: she had very fine eyes,
And her talk was a mixture of foolish and wise.
Her adorers were many, and one of them said,
"She waltzed rather well! It's a pity she's dead!"

George John Cayley

4

In order to understand the process of dying, it is necessary to understand the make-up of man.

Man's beautifully complicated body is so designed that countless functions overlap. Practically every action has a reaction; sometimes causing, in turn, another action and reaction.

The reason is that man is a multicellular creature. That is, he is made up of many cells, each with a different function. Some are more highly specialized than others. Because of this specialization, not all cells die at the same time.

Perhaps our body could be compared to an automobile assembly line. As the chassis moves along, various parts are attached. Some of the parts are absolutely necessary for the automobile to perform its designed function.

Certainly without an engine the car couldn't be driven out of the back door of the factory. It could, however, get along without a dome light. The human could get along without an eye but he certainly couldn't get far without a heart. Just ask the Tin Man in the Wizard of Oz!

As the car ages, the upholstery may wear out and not be replaced—or the floor mats discarded from rough usage. These are specialized and may receive rougher handling and so "die" first.

There are three forms of death in any multicellular animal which we will discuss.

The death of certain cells, which are replaced by new cells, is known as necrobiosis. This form of death occurs in the normal course of body activity. Peeling after sun-burn is an example. The outer burned layer sloughs off and is replaced by new fresh skin.

Another form is necrosis. This is the death of a group of cells that are not replaced by living tissue.

Death of heart tissue in a non-fatal heart attack could be cited as an example of necrosis.

Somatic death is the third form--the death of the entire organism. This is the ultimate and inevitable stage of all living animals.

SOMATIC DEATH

There are three systems necessary to sustain life in the human body. Certainly one is no more important than the other. These are the respiratory system, the cardiovascular system and the central nervous system. Failure of any one of these leads eventually to death.

Basic to the proper function of these systems is the circulation of the blood. Since the blood carries the nutrients to cells, failure of this causes immediate death!

As the blood ceases to flow, the tissues begin irreversible changes. Cells within the highly developed organs die. The march toward complete cellular death has begun. Not until all cells are dead, and this may take several hours, is somatic death complete.

Death is something difficult to detect with complete finality. More than once a doctor has been called by a mortician at the funeral home with a statement similar to "Dr. X, your patient Mr. Smith says he would like to go home."

However, in the vast majority of cases there is no doubt that death has arrived. There are many tests that can be made to assure this.

Among the most obvious indications of finality are the cessation of any heartbeat and lack of lung activity. This is known as clinical death or "legal death." Although a person has reached this stage, he oftentimes may be brought back to life. It is during this period that "life-after-death" experiences have been recalled.

If the period extends beyond a reasonable time, the cells in certain brain areas die and normal mentality is lost forever. This reasonable time may vary according to many conditions. Suffice to say that a period much longer than 6 minutes will lead to irreparable damage.

Beyond this point, death is irreversible. Critical cells within the central nervous system have ceased to function. Tissues are being attacked by autolytic digestion.

This is the self-digestion of body tissues by the products of these tissues. These products or enzymes, in life, aid in the digestion and metabolism of nutrients delivered to the cells. After death, they continue to do their dedicated job. Only they no longer have nutrients to digest, so they digest the cell in which they were produced.

When all cells have ceased activity, final or somatic death has been attained. This may not occur for an hour or two (occasionally up to six hours) after respiration and heart action stops. The patient, however, ceased living after brain death.

PEACEFUL DEATH

The vast majority of deaths are peaceful. The patient stops breathing. Shortly thereafter, or often simultaneously, the heart action stops. The body relaxes and the lower jaw drops. The eyes may fail to close. Soon the brain cells start dying. The major organs cease to function.

Depending on environmental conditions, such as temperature and humidity or on the nature of death, secondary changes result within a relatively short time.

This includes a gradual cooling of the body called algor mortis. The muscles become rigid and stiff which is known as rigor mortis. Tissue discoloration due to settling blood is referred to as livor mortis. Clotting of blood, dessecation of body parts and putrefaction complete the decomposing process. These will be covered more thoroughly in another chapter.

IS DEATH NECESSARY?

Death may be considered from different points of view. From the purely physiological viewpoint, it is the ceasing of protoplasmic activity within the body cells. In other words, when the cells cease to convert nutrients to maintain life, then the cell dies. Our body being made of trillions of cells dies gradually. We start to die from the moment we are born. We do not finish the dying process until all cells are dead.

The majority of deaths are from illness and accidents. The only natural death is from old age. Most of our cells do not have the ability to divide indefinitely. The renewal of cells slows down and eventually ceases. In the young, these cells are constantly being renewed; in the elderly this is not the case. As a result, when illness strikes, the elderly are not as apt to weather the cellular destruction. The body cannot fight off the illness and succumbs.

As scientists work toward the rejuvenation of cells, the elderly may increase their life span threefold. Many may live the long lives of Biblical times.

We must recognize, therefore, that death is necessary. This is in order to make the appearance of new individuals and species possible.

Not only human life but all life, is made from cells. Plants, animals and humans are constructed from atoms which form the cells. As the cells die, new ones are formed. Eventually this process ceases.

When all cells die and the body decomposes, the atoms are not destroyed. They find their way into the soil (or air in the case of cremation) and are reused by plants which may eventually be eaten by humans. So these atoms may again become a part of a human. Could this be the reincarnation referred to by many religions?

To make death unnecessary, reproduction would have to cease. Growth and evolution would then cease.

So in an evolutionary universe such as ours, death is a necessity.

5

THE FINAL FAILURE

COMMON SENSE

"There's been an accident!" they said,
"Your servant's cut in half; he's dead!"
"Indeed!" said Mr. Jones, "and please
Send me the half that's got the keys."

Harry Graham

5

The three necessary life sustaining systems each rely on one vital organ for existence. The respiratory system relies on the lungs through which the body absorbs oxygen. The cardiovascular system has the heart and the central nervous system is controlled by the brain. Failure of any one of these will result in death.

HEART FAILURE

Cardiac failure may result from a number of causes. The heart requires oxygenated blood in a certain quantity. If the quantity falls below a certain level, due to hemorrhage from a severed blood vessel or large organ rupture, the heart will cease to function.

Likewise if the heart does not receive certain stimuli due to an injury or desease, it will cease. This could occur from shock, poisons, body blows on head or chest, or its own abnormal actions. Fibrillation of the heart muscle is an example of this.

Fibrillation or quivering of muscle fibers if occurring in the ventricles, prevents blood from being expelled from the heart. This is probably the immediate cause of death in many diseases where the heart suddenly fails. This most certainly occurs in electrocution deaths where the passage of electric currents alters the normal electrical stimuli to the heart.

BRAIN FAILURE

Though we do not often refer to the brain's cessation of activity as "brain failure," it certainly states clearly one cause of death.

An injury to the brain as a result of a concussion or skull fracture can lead to a coma. Meningitis, embolisms, uremic or alcoholic poisoning can also cause a fatal coma.

As the coma deepens, respiration slows down gradually. The circulatory system follows this decline in activity. Finally the patient dies from lack of oxygen in the blood which no longer allows the heart to sustain life. The rectal sphincter muscle relaxes often with a resultant waste discharge. The collected mucous in the throat may create a "death rattle" from the final laborious breaths.

In the event of "instant" death due to a crushing skull injury, the impulses to the heart and lung cease.

A chicken with its head cut off may still move for a length of time. There is a tale or legend that the Huns did similar things to humans. Wagers were made how many steps a man would run if his head were cleanly severed from his body **the instant** his executor yelled "run!" Supposedly it was up to five or six steps before the headless body collapsed to earth.

It has been noticed that in an accidental decapitation the heart may beat strongly sending powerful squirts of blood through the carotid arteries. This occurs for only a short duration but does indicate a heart function independent from the brain activity.

LUNG FAILURE

Lung failure results from the inability of oxygen to reach the lungs. Anything that blocks or strangulates the trachea (windpipe) or air breathing apparatus prevents this vital gas from reaching its life-giving destination.

Many people are not aware that a drowning person is actually suffocating. It is usually thought that he (or she) breathes in water, filling the lungs with water and causing death.

In reality very little water enters the lungs of a drowning victim. At the first sign of a foreign substance entering the trachea, the epiglottis clamps tightly shut refusing intrusion of anything--including air. Thus breathing is prevented and the hapless victim suffocates. Autopsies invariably reveal no more than a tablespoon of water in the lungs. This is not true of the stomach however, as the struggling person gulps considerable quantities in his fruitless attempt to survive.

Another example of suffocation is hanging or strangling. Here again the air is cut off to the lungs. Paralysis of respiratory muscles and diseases such as pneumonia and emphysema are other causes.

Without oxygen in the lungs, to be carried by the blood to other tissues, cellular death is certain.

6

LOOK INTO MY EYE

LUCY LAKE

Poor Lucy Lake was overgrown,
But somewhat underbrained.
She did not know enough, I own,
To go in when it rained.

Yet Lucy was constrained to go;
Green bedding,--you infer.
Few people knew she died, but oh,
The difference to her!

Newton Mackintosh

6

Private eyes in detective shows reach down and press the carotid artery in the neck. "He's dead" they pronounce expertly. "Let's go after the killer" and they dash out of the house after the culprit.

The doctors on M*A*S*H go considerably further. Using their stethoscope they listen for bronchial sounds. Pressing it against the chest or trachea, they listen for a heartbeat or sound of air movement. They lift the eyelid and check the look of the eye.

Looking through their ophthalmoscope they check for movement of blood in the fine capillaries in the back of the eye. They check for dilation of the pupil. If both tests are negative, the patient is probably dead.

This is not positive, because in some disorders these tests may not give proof of death.

Not having access to sophisticated hospital equipment, how can the average individual detect death? There are various ways that have a basis in science.

Applying heat, such as from a candle or match, directly to the skin will cause a blister if the patient is still alive. If not, the skin will separate in layers.

Tying off the end of a finger is an ancient but tested means of determining death by the layman. In a living person the end will swell and discolor.

The medically untutored might check for the cessation of respiration in the following ways. Hold a mirror in front of the nose and/or mouth as a check for moisture condensation. A feather placed in the nostril may also detect air movement. Neither of these tests is conclusive as other factors may cause condensation or air movement.

Placing the ear next to the chest to hear the sound of a heart beat might aid in determining death. Naturally the use of a stethoscope is the more professional way.

The circulation of the blood ceases when the heart stops. Blood flow, as mentioned before, may be detected with an ophthalmoscope. Without one, the layman might place the patients' hand near a strong light. The opaqueness of the webs between the fingers may indicate that blood has ceased to flow.

Thus death may be determined by the layman through careful observation. Absence of breathing and heartbeat for at least 20 minutes is one indicator. A strong light flashed in the dilated eyes will usually cause the pupils to contract in a living person. This is not the case in the dead. Touching the sensitive cornea (the transparent covering of the front of the eyeball) will precipitate no reaction in the deceased.

Later the cornea loses its transparency. It turns milky and becomes wrinkled. The body begins to cool and rigor mortis begins.

The eye, then is the window of the mind in the living and the transom through which death can be seen in the lifeless.

7

XAXOS, THE MUMMY

ELEGY

The jackals prowl, the serpents hiss
In what was once Persepolis.
Proud Babylon is but a trace
Upon the desert's dusty face.
The topless towers of Ilium
Are ashes. Judah's harp is dumb.
The fleets of Ninevah and Tyre
Are down with Davy Jones, Esquire
And all the oligarchies, kings,
And potentates that ruled these things
Are gone! But cheer up; don't be sad;
Think what a lovely time they had!

Arthur Guiterman

7

Embalming extends back in time thousands of years. The successful embalmers of the past chiefly used the principle of dehydration. All moisture from the body was removed so that there would be no fatty tissue to decompose.

This dehydration process occurred over a long period of time. In the case of the Canary Island Guanches (descendants of Ham) the body was allowed to dry-out for seventy days. This was a long period between death and funeral. Possibly because of the hotter, drier climate in Egypt, the period was only forty days. After this extended period the mummified body, or Xaxos, was wrapped inside pouches made from goat skins.

One of the chief aims of the Guanches was to prepare for death. All throughout life they collected and treated goat skins for their final entombment.

Preparing the corpses for embalming was a lonely profession. The "prepar-ors" could care less whether the "prepar-ees" were considered contaminated and thus lived a secluded and unmolested life in extreme solitude.

Organs from the wealthy were removed, soaked in wine and sealed in marked containers. The poor, unable to afford these extras, did not have the benefits of this ritual. The body was bathed in wines, filled with herbs and balsam and dried in a hot oven or under the sun.

After dressing in proper raiment befitting the person's station in life, he was secretly entombed in a casket concealed from animals and human vandals. The body was being preserved for the return of the spirit which had left its home for a few thousand years.

Their method of embalming served the dead; the modern method serves the living.

Instead of dehydrating the body, the modern embalmer attempts to prevent fluids from rapidly leaving the body and changing its countenance. At the same time, he attempts to prevent or cover odors produced by the decomposing body. Probably this was the purpose of the wine in the Guanches and early Egyptian rituals. The aromatics used contained ether which aided in dehydration and the final bony, leather-like appearance.

The modern day method of embalming is far superior to the Egyptian way. The "secret" of their embalming is known to morticians but is discarded for obvious reasons. The purpose then, as mentioned before, was to preserve for thousands of years. The purpose now is to preserve from death to internment--a few days at most.

Embalming, more or less as we know it today, began during the Civil War to prepare the dead soldiers for shipment to their home burial grounds. Prior to this war, soldiers fallen on the battlefield were buried where they fell--or in a nearby cemetery. With the advent of embalming, the dead soldiers could be shipped home for the first time for burial in their family plot. The prevention of putrefaction and its resultant obnoxious odor allowed the deceased's relatives to attend the funeral-- even from a distant point.

The embalmers discovered they were not only doing a service to the loved ones back home, but also that there was a profit to be made.

8

THE ADEQUATE AQUADUCT

Said I, kneeling, as the Pope passed by:
"There, but for the grace of God, go I."

Victor Buono

8

The human body is made up of thousands of miles of capillaries fed by arteries. These capillaries are small enough to allow direct nourishment of cells by the life-carrying blood. The blood returns to the heart through veins which gradually increase in size until it flows into a main vein.

This remarkable system may be compared to a city's water supply and sewage removal. As the water leaves the pumping station, large mains carry the flow. As the branches divide into streets the pipes get smaller. The feeders into the home are still smaller and the faucet to the sink is the smallest of all.

As the sewage exits the house it joins a larger sewer drain. This in turn unites with a bigger pipe to carry the offals from several blocks. Finally the waste is dumped or fed to its eventual destination.

At any particular time, because of the required use by a certain home, the system may have less water flowing in it than some other part.

This is likewise true in the human body. Did you ever feel cool after eating? The blood is rushing to your stomach and digestive organs and leaving your skin surface.

Throughout your body, at any particular time, about 50% of your capillaries are not calling for blood to feed the tissues. So, at death, embalming fluid may be pumped into the system faster than the blood is drained out.

As the minute capillaries are filled, the fluid hopefully seeps into the surrounding tissues. Just as the heart pumps with pressure, so, too, does the mechanical injector work under pressure. This forces the fluid into the capillaries, working against the back pressure of stagnant clotted blood and tissue resistance. Unfortunately not all points can be reached, in many cases, because of fatal factors such as mutilation, disease, or other blockages. In such cases it is necessary to make a localized opening and feed the fluid through smaller arteries or its branches.

It takes many gallons of embalming fluid to adequately reach all the tissue in the 47,000 square feet of body tissue in the average adult. In many cases not all points in the body are reached. A lengthy exposure at room temperature may start the area to turn green.

Without complications, the embalming fluid is pumped through the arterial system with relative ease. It is drained from the accompanying trunk vein.

With complications, localized insertion of fluid and localized blood removal may be necessary.

9

I KNEW YOU WOULD CHANGE

LINES WRITTEN AFTER A BATTLE
By an assistant surgeon of the Nineteenth Nankeens

Stiff are the warrior's muscles,
Congeal'd, alas! his chyle;
No more in hostile tussles
Will he excite his bile.
Dry is the epidermis,
A vein no longer bleeds--
And the communis vermis
Upon the warrior feeds.

Compress'd, alas! the thorax,
That throbbed with joy or pain;
Not e'en a dose of borax
Could make it throb again.
Dried up the warrior's throat is,
All shatter'd too, his head;
Still is the epiglottis--
The warrior is dead.

Unknown

9

Our body, in life as well as death, is crawling with millions of organisms. If one could see under a high-powered microscope he would be amazed at the number and kinds of parasites clinging to and living on our body.

A large number of these are within our digestive system. A new-born baby is germ-free for the first minutes of life. Shortly after taking its first breath it becomes germ-laden like the rest of us.

Our natural body makeup fights these organisms constantly during life. At death our defenses cease and the organisms begin to take over.

AUTOLYSIS

Autolysis is the destruction of tissues by bacteria produced within those tissues. Each body cell contains elements within capable of the destruction of that cell. These agents or enzymes are able to digest a million times their own weight. Anti-enzymes formed within the body combat this activity during life, but cease at death.

After death these enzymes begin their eventual de-struction and decomposition. It is common to use formal-dehyde in embalming fluid to weaken the enzyme action and thus slow down their self-destruction.

CADAVERIC SPASMS

At death the muscles become flaccid. Later as rigor develops, they harden.

In certain types of death, such as suicide or acci-dent, where the person is under great strees, the muscles mysteriously tighten into a final death grip. A gun in the hand may be practically impossible to pry loose from a suicide's grasp.

The final death spasm is not rigor mortis, but this eventually follows.

A drowning person may clutch a stick or board; a parachutist may have his chute lines in an unbreakable hold. A soldier killed in the trenches may still cling tenaciously to his weapon immediately following death.

ALGOR MORTIS

Under normal conditions, a nude body cools at the approximate rate of one degree per hour (four degrees per hour the first few hours)--if dead, of course. After about 40 hours the interior temperature taken rectally equals the ambient temperature.

Naturally, surrounding temperatures would vary this somewhat--as would extra layers of fat on an obese corpse.

Without the body's cooling system operating, occasionally a high temperature of short duration may be observed immediately following death. Probable causes are certain infectious diseases.

RIGOR MORTIS

This stiffening process first begins in the involuntary muscles, such as the heart. Beginning usually within twelve hours (and often more like eight) after death, it generally lasts three or four days.

First visible in the eyelids and jaw muscles, it moves progressively down the neck and throughout the muscles of the body.

Often the arms are the last to become rigid. Here again, temperature affects its onset. Cold retards it and warmth hastens it.

The more rapidly rigor mortis begins, the longer it usually lasts. More heavily muscled bodies, such as athletes and weight lifters, are likely to show early rigor.

Once the rigidity has been broken, it does not return. The muscles return to the flaccid condition they were prior to rigor setting in. Massage, bending and manipulating the extremities by the mortician aids in breaking up this condition.

Where precipitation of protein causes it, increasing acidity in the muscles leads to the loss of it.

LIVOR MORTIS

As blood settles after the cessation of the heart, it leads to a discoloration in the dependent parts of the body.

If the body were moved, blood would slowly flow to the lowest body area. Thus a detective, coroner or doctor can usually tell if death occurred at the location where the body was discovered.

BLOOD CLOTTING

In many instances, clotting begins even before death--particularly in deaths from lung diseases where the blood has been unable to get enough oxygen. After death the blood coagulates with all its elements into a jelly-like consistency.

In a slow death for instance, the red blood cells may separate and being heavier sink to the lower part of the clot. The leukocytes (mainly white cells) rise to the top.

DESSICATION

The drying of certain parts, such as the cornea of the eye, is usually a sure indication of death. As the fluids sink to the back of the eye, the cornea dries out, glazes over and becomes wrinkled.

This dryness may also be observed over abrasions or wounds. The lips also become hard and reddish-black in color.

PUTREFACTION

There are certain bacterial organisms within the intestinal canal that multiply rapidly upon the death of their host. These organisms enter the tissues, softening and decomposing them.

One of the results is a foul-smelling gas—hydrogen sulfide which has the odor of rotten eggs. Other gases produced may alter the body pigmentation and turn it various colors, the most frequent of which is green. This usually occurs first in the right lower quadrant of the abdomen.

Bodies kept below 32 degrees F, will not putrefy as long as they remain frozen. The less moisture present, the slower the putrefacation process. It occurs more rapidly in babies, mutilated, and obese individuals and patients succumbing to such diseases as typhoid and septicemia (bacteria growing in the blood stream).

10

IS EMBALMING NECESSARY?

EXISTENTIALISM

I'm tired of trying to think;
I think I shall simply behave.
Behavior may drive you to drink
But it's thinking that leads to the grave.

Lloyd Frankenberg

10

Probably there is no room in the labyrinth of a funeral home less understood by the layman than the "embalming" room. In this barren area with its inevitable floor drain, the mortician works with consummate skill to transform the dead into life-like corpses. What a paradox!

Although we assume the best compliment that can be paid a mortician is to say of the deceased, "He looks just as if he were sleeping," this is not so. In actuality the skilled mortician attempts to give the body the appearance of peaceful repose; an image half-way between sleeping and dead.

The preparation room has its own air-conditioning unit to exhaust odors and gases completely, and not let them co-mingle with other exhaust systems.

A body lift, either mechanical or electrical, aids in lifting the cadaver from the table and placing it in the casket.

The table, cold and hard, is surrounded by a gutter into which flow disinfectants, soap suds, whiskers, hair clippings and other body residue. The table may be tilted to aid in preparation.

At the end of the table sits an embalming machine. To the tubes issuing from it are connected various instruments to insert fluid into the body.

A medical cabinet holds an assortment of tools including medical scalpels, forceps, hemostats, needle holders, clamps and sutures. Additional instruments include vein tubes, jugular tubes, mouth formers, aspirators, cavity injectors, cranial trocars, eye caps and assorted abdominal trocars. Many instruments are specialized and manufactured only for this trade.

Jars, bottles and containers of chemicals are in sight. As a nurse uses a disinfectant to clean the arm before a hypodermic injection, so do morticians use it in their battle against bacterial decomposition. Such disinfectants as corgolic acid, cresol, lysol, formalin, iodine and ethyl alcohol are commonly found around a preparation room.

THREE OBJECTIVES

There are three objectives to modern embalming: (1) Sterilization for the protection of the living; (2) Preservation and (3) Bringing comfort to the bereaved by restoring and recreating life-like features through techniques and cosmetics.

In order to stop the decomposition process, embalming should be done within eight hours after death. It is usually routinely performed as part of the total burial service. The allows the body to be viewed lying-in-state and avoids embarrassing odors emanating from the decomposing body.

Neither the Christian nor Jewish religions require embalming, but it has become a practice through custom and tradition. Although it is not common outside the United States and Canada, it is gradually being accepted in some countries.

It is claimed it is psychologically healthy for the mourners to view the deceased. Because people tend to deny unpleasant reality, it sets positively in a person's mind that the loved one will never again be seen on earth. The mind then adjusts and starts to cope with the grief involved.

The author recalls attending the closed-casket funeral of a good friend who had been incinerated in an automobile accident. Obviously there was no body to view.

The author has seen countless times in a crowd, the familiar shoulders and head of this powerfully built man-- only to discover upon turning that the face was entirely different. Had the body been viewed, this comparison undoubtedly would not exist.

Contrary to popular belief, embalming is not required by law in the United States except under certain conditions. It is required if the body is to be transported to another location aboard a common carrier. This is certainly a logical law as the body begins decomposing very shortly after death. Because of the fear of plagues and public health protection, death from a communicable disease requires this process.

In many states, if the body is to be held for a certain period of time, it is required to be embalmed--or at the very least, refrigerated. In other states it is mandatory that the body be embalmed if there is to be public viewing permitted.

Viewing can be accomplished with refrigeration alone, in some states, providing the body is not out of the refrigerated facilities for more than two or three hours at a time. Of course the body in this situation will feel undesirably cold to the touch.

Cadavers for medical school use, which may last up to nine months, are embalmed with about seven gallons of fluid--considerably more than usual. Just as we used to dissect frogs in high school which were preserved in formaldehyde, so are these cadavers preserved. Also used is carbolic acid which deters the formation of mold. To keep the bodies moist, glycerine is also injected along with the above.

In the old days, embalming could take several days to complete since the fluids were not forced in under pressure. Through the use of gravity, the fluid seeped into all parts from a small incision in the groin.

If embalming is not done and if there is no available refrigeration for the body, it may be placed in a heavy plastic pouch within the casket. Of course there would be no viewing in this instance.

TRIAL AND ERROR

As in all professions, perfection was not obtained immediately. Through co-operation of chemical manufacturing concerns, discontent of loved ones and the desire of perfectionists embalming gradually improved to its present state of the art.

At the turn of this century, tissues were made hard by chemicals which coagulated blood near the surface and created a putty color. Touching a corpse was like touching marble--hard and cold.

Attempting to soften tissues, using less fluid, ended in improper embalming. By continuing experimentation, the proper methods were developed.

Problems are exacerbated since no two bodies are alike--in life or in death. What might work properly for one could be an under or over-dose to another.

In the living, the physician starts with a minimum dose and alters it depending on the reaction from his patient. The mortician thoroughly studies pathological conditions in the dead body to get the proper reaction.

The problem he faces varies according to the cause of death: if by disease it is helpful to know the pre-death condition and its complication. Knowledge of these conditions aids in analyzing the problems to be overcome by the embalming fluid--and there can be many. More will be covered on this in another chapter.

So is embalming necessary? Except for certain conditions previously stated, it becomes for the most part, a personal choice by the decedent's family.

11

SECRETS OF EMBALMING

Morden W. Chicklett, the chewing gum heir, died today. In accordance with his wishes, he will be cremated and his ashes will be stuck to a chair in a nearby restaurant!

Steve Allen Show, 1981

11

Embalming may be divided into two separate procedures. The first is to replace the blood supply with an embalming fluid containing, among other things, formaldehyde.

The second, and an equally important process, is removing the viscera fluids in the chest and abdominal cavities and injecting in its place, a preservative.

THE MORTICIAN BEGINS

After donning a pair of protective gloves, the mortician removes the clothes of the deceased. Care is exercised so that the body is not roughly handled which could lead to problems later. The modesty of the deceased is protected by placing a covering over certain exposed areas.

If rigor mortis has begun, the muscles need to be returned to a flaccid condition. By massaging, bending and manipulating the extremities, the mortician breaks up this condition.

The body is then cleansed with a disinfectant soap. A good lather should be produced and all parts of the body thoroughly cleaned. Germs and foreign matter will thus be removed from the skin.

The body is then sprayed with a disinfectant and the orifices are packed to prevent leakage. They are first swabbed with cavity fluid.

After towel drying, a massage cream is applied to the hands and face. Massaging lightly is necessary at this point. Heavy massaging, if facial cyanosis is present, could break down the structure of the blood's red cells and free hemoglobin. The cyanosis or blue condition of the blood could pass in the hemoglobin through the capillary walls into the tissues and covert blood discoloration into blood staining of the skin.

The nostrils, mouth and throat are treated with a good disinfectant. False teeth (if used) are inserted, the mouth is closed and stitched.

To demonstrate advances made in the last two or three decades, the original mouth stitching was made as follows:

A one-inch stitch was made in the deep tissues of the lower lips; a similar stitch was made in the upper lip. The needle was then inserted through the roof of the mouth exiting at the nostril. It was re-inserted through the septum (the dividing wall between the nostrils), down into the mouth cavity again and tied sufficiently tight to make the lips look natural.

Now, however, a simple wire with a hooked barb on one end is inserted in the upper gum line and pressed into the tissue. Similarly, another is inserted in the lower gum line. The two wires are then joined and the mouth pulled closed. It is much quicker, more efficient and aesthetically much neater.

The face is shaved clean. It is necessary to be careful as a nick will turn brown from exposure to the drying effect of air.

The eyeballs are washed with a mild solution as eyelids are extremely sensitive to chemicals. An eyecup, with small protrusions to engage the underside of the eyelid, are inserted. These are made in two sizes and oval or round shape. The lids are closed so the upper lid is two-thirds over the eye and the lower lid is brought up the other one-third to allow them to just touch--and not to overlap.

The facial muscles which tend to sag in age, are lifted to improve on the naturalness people want when viewing their dead.

The body is positioned in a straight line with the head end elevated slightly to permit drainage. If it is out of line, the head may not lay properly on the pillow when positioned later. It will stubbornly refuse to center itself, but instead rest on the front or back half.

With the constant research and development of chemical companies, new and sophisticated embalming fluids are being developed. The glutaraldehydes aid in preventing the muscles from rigidly setting up and thus allow slight movement of the protein in the cells. Prior to the use of these chemicals, the body position would set rapidly and become difficult to change. Thus big toes were tied together to keep the legs in line. In large breasted women, the breasts were sutured close to the nipples and pulled together to hold them in the proper position.

The hands are positioned with left over the right. They are cupped with the fingers in a natural curved arc.

LOCATING THE ARTERIES

The proper artery or arteries to use for the injection are picked after careful study. The ones selected should allow an easy approach, concealment of incision, large enough for instrument insertion and superficial enough to avoid unnecessary dissection. Severed arteries that were caused by an accidental death are ligated or tied off with a string or thread. This prevents leakage of embalming fluid.

Once the arteries are decided upon, a cut is made and the artery brought to the surface. An object such as a tongue depresser is placed under the artery to hold it above the skin surface and allow an instrument insertion for blood removal.

The important arteries are located along lineal guides. The main neck artery, the carotid, follows a line midway between the ear lobe and the lower jawbone to the junction of the collar and breast bone. Injecting fluid at this point distributes it throughout the entire side of the head internally as well as externally, above the point of injection.

Injecting both carotid arteries at the same time ensures distributing fluid throughout the head at the same moment. This allows the same expression, the same degree of reaction and the same change on both sides of the face and head.

The axillary artery in the shoulder area continues to the brachial artery in the upper arm. The guides for this are the bicep and tricep muscles. Since it is sheathed with the vein and nerve, it is necessary to split the sheath to have access to it.

One of the most used arteries, along with the axillary/brachial and carotid openings for pumping in embalming fluid, is the iliac artery. The guides are the hip bone and the pubic bone, between which it lies. The iliac artery goes through the thigh becoming then the femoral artery.

The femoral artery continues down the leg branching near the knee into the posterior tibial and the peronaeal that takes blood to the calf and lower areas. Likewise the brachial artery in the upper arm branches into the radial and the ulnar which serves the forearm and wrist areas.

The embalmer's "six points" for injection, then, are the right and left carotid, right and left axillary and the right and left iliac or femoral arteries. The corresponding veins at these points are likewise used for blood drainage.

THE IDIOSYNCRASES OF BLOOD

At death and upon the cessation of the pumping action of the heart, blood seeks the lowest level—due to its specific gravity. As the heart weakens and the left ventricle ceases its pumping action, the walls of the arteries are no longer strong enough to send the blood back from the veins. As a result the arteries are usually emptied of blood before actual somatic death. Blood then is massed within the large truck veins and within the right side of the heart. As the blood no longer moves, decomposition begins.

The heavier fibrin moves to the lower levels and a lighter fluid is moved to the upper levels. This fibrin coagulates to form blood clots. High temperatures within the body hasten this coagulation.

Death from carbon monoxide gas poisoning, for example, will slow the process. The blood will remain liquid and scarlet for a long time.

Carbon dioxide accumulation, as in pneumonia which restricts oxygen absorption, leaves the blood very dark and forms a jelly-like mass near death.

It is difficult if not impractical to dissolve blood clots after death. They may be arrested in forming, if shortly after death, glycerine solutions are arterially injected.

As nature takes its inevitable course toward decomposition, liquid tissues, as blood, start first. After the fibrin separates, the liquids seek exit from the body.

The dark blood discoloration in the vessels is reflected through the skin. If pressure is placed and then released on a part of the body where this occurs and the discoloration is cleared, it is still within the vessel. If it doesn't, then it has carried through the vessel wall into the tissue and has stained it. Short of bleaching this post-mortem stain and covering it with makeup, there is not much that can be done to conceal it.

BLOOD REMOVAL

To achieve good results, it is necessary to remove as much blood as possible--not leaving a large mass in any one area. Practically it is nearly impossible to remove all the blood. Any left in considerable quantity may discolor the surrounding tissues.

The fluid, to be injected arterially, must reach enough of the surrounding tissue to do a good job of embalming. This is injected under pressure in a large enough volume to reach the sub-arteries and the capillaries. The blood is drained through the veins allowing the fluid to replace congested blood with its accompanying facial discoloration.

To prevent the formaldehyde-based fluid from coming into contact with the chemically-charged blood and causing cosmetic changes, a pre-injection solution is used. For instance, in a jaundiced death the skin bile pigment in blood may cause the tissues to change from its characteristic yellow to green if this pre-injection solution were not used.

The arterial system is not always free of blood after death. This is particularly true in "sudden" death where the heart stops instantly. In drawing from such an artery it is wise to wash out, as much as possible, this arterial blood with pre-injection solution.

As blood decomposes, gas forms. This bubbles out in draining. Occasionally a stoppage in draining occurs when a blood clot prevents further action. If too much pressure is used to inject fluid and a clot blocks it, distension of tissues result.

After surgery, where the medical team used coagulants to encourage clotting, the blood is jelly-like and dark. It resists removal. To use a solvent and dissolve the clots requires oxygen which is seldom found in sufficient quantity to accomplish this.

In deaths from heart conditions there is usually considerable water in the tissues. Thus, the drawing of the blood is usually accomplished with relative ease. Through the process of osmosis the water passes into the capillaries, thus balancing the water content and giving a more natural appearance to the tissues.

Dry tissues attract moisture through the capillary membrane; moist tissues force movement into them and is carried away through the veins. High temperature before death often creates this dried, rapid decomposition and subsequent poisonous liquids and gases in the system. These may react adversely to the injection of embalming fluids.

Since the reflex centers do not die immediately, an injection of cold, warm or strong fluids may cause a noticeable muscular movement. This could startle a novice embalmer working alone in his laboratory at night!

These contractions are in response to the reflex nerve centers that are still alive.

CAVITY TREATMENT

Following arterial injection, it is necessary to remove from the body cavities the blood, fluid and accumulated gases.

A long, hollow and pointed instrument, called a trocar, is inserted into the abdomen above and to the left of the navel. It is pushed upward through the upper area of the diaphragm and turned downward to reach the fluid. It withdraws the contents of organs which more rapidly tend to decompose. It is then swung around, outside the lung area, to reach the different levels.

The trocar is connected to either an electric or hydro-aspirator hose. With the use of suction, it withdraws fluids from the body and exits them down the drain.

The embalming machine then pumps embalming preservatives throughout the body. It contains two and a half gallons and can be pumped under constant pressure or under intermittent pulsating action. This pulsating action may be necessary at times to dislodge blood clots from the circulatory system. Both pressure and rate of flow may be controlled.

After the body has been embalmed, it is once more bathed. The hair is washed and dried. The nails are manicured. Cosmetics are applied to visible areas to restore natural coloring.

The body is then dressed completely and placed in the casket for viewing.

Although the mortician could stand in the background and listen proudly to the comments being made about his handiwork, he is busying himself taking care of the needs of the bereaved.

12

WANT SOMETHING SPECIAL?

AN EPITAPH INTENDED FOR HIS WIFE

Here lies my wife: here let her lie!
Now she's at rest, and so am I.

John Dryden

12

Upon learning that the loved one has "crossed over," a phone call to the mortician usually follows. Information is passed regarding location of body, cause of death, etc. The mortician then takes charge.

A great many people die in the hospital. If a person dies elsewhere the body is often brought to a hospital for death confirmation. That's why so many obituaries read DOA or "dead on arrival" at the hospital.

Transportation from the hospital to a mortuary is quickly arranged. The body may not be removed, by law, without the decedent's family's consent. Once consent is given the body is removed so that embalming may begin as quickly as possible.

A call on the mortician aids in expediting the details for the funeral. Considerable paperwork is necessary in many cases to claim death benefits. Among these forms are the death certificate, copies of birth certificates, copies of marriage certificate, copies of W-2 forms or income tax returns and veterans discharge papers.

Realizing that it may take several months to collect death benefits and pay funeral costs, morticians often allow a three to four months interest-free grace period for payment. Since they have a considerable sum involved, they must start charging interest after that period.

Many funeral homes offer a delayed payment plan. Since a sudden death to the money-earner may catch a family unawares, arrangements are often made to pay the funeral costs on an installment basis.

Inasmuch as we only die once, our loved ones are usually inexperienced in making funeral arrangements. We depend a great deal on the advice of the funeral director--and rightly so. After all, he is the "pro" and can answer the questions and guide us expertly every step of the way.

At many mortuaries, extras may be offered to make the service a memorable one.

Larger funerals may include a special flower car to carry the displays to the cemetery. Extra limousines carry the immediate family as well as pall-bearers, in-laws and the clergy. This may be preceded by a motorcycle escort to keep the road clear for the procession.

Often Jewish families do not have a shroud to drape over the casket. This can be furnished by most morticians.

In cases where a person drowns, was an accident victim or shows the ravages of an extended illness, the casket is kept closed to the mourners. The funeral director may suggest a photograph be placed on the closed casket surrounded by appropriate wreaths and other expressions of condolence. This offers some solace, but psychologically, actual viewing of the body helps more quickly to accept its finality.

Death masks of many famous personages grace our museums. Plaster casts capture for perpetuity their actual features. In some mortuaries, a similar service can be performed for a loved one.

Of course, a register with the visitor's signatures, is a treasure to pour over later. Memories flood back of the concern and love expressed by friends, relatives and even casual acquaintances who took the time our of their lives to pay their last respects.

Other services offered by the director include hired pallbearers, in case the deceased is aged and his contemporaries have preceded him.

If he is a veteran or member of a fraternal order, the flag or apron (Masonic) displayed on his casket can be mounted in a permanent memorial case.

It is advisable if one passes away in a town different from where he is to be buried that the family calls the mortician in his home town. He will make the necessary arrangements with the local undertaker.

In large cities the placement of an obituary in the local paper is handled by the mortician. The newspapers usually charge a fee for printing it. One of the advantages of a small town is that the death notice is automatically picked up by the local newspaper from public records and printed without charge as local news.

Besides the professional services handled by the mortician, many of them have complete libraries of books dealing with the subject of death and how to handle it. They are often allied with the local library and will graciously lend the books on request.

Many of the more enlightened mortuaries include on their staff a trained grief counselor who co-ordinates the bereavement follow-up procedures. The counselor offers invaluable assistance and aid to help the family accept its loss.

The funeral director, being the trained and accomplished professional that he is, will handle details with dignity and honesty. He has learned that contrary to the traditional delicacy in the discussion of death, the modern view of "tell it like it is" also applies. This is not to say that he is tasteless or crass in discussing final arrangements, but his discussion and recommendations will be couched in understanding dialogue. Grief cannot be glossed over nor can its reality be denied.

In describing final procedures, his explanation may follow along these lines:

"Mrs. Smith, we are taking every care to prepare your husband for final viewing. Your friends may visit with you here tomorrow evening after 7:00. Service will be held the following morning at 10:00 after which we will proceed to Memory Gardens for the internment service. We feel confident that in your bereavement, you and your friends will cherish these last moments and will remember them with the same dignity that characterized his life."

If something special is wanted in the service, a discussion with the funeral director will usually get it accomplished. He will do his best to be accommodating.

13

A BANG, A SLIT

AND A SIGH

IT'S THREE NO TRUMP

"It's three no trump," the soldier said;
A sniper's bullet struck him dead.
His cards bedecked the trench's bottom.
A comrade peered--"Yes, he'd 'a' got 'em!"

Guy Innes

13

Perhaps parents do have the right to complain! There is a lot of violence shown on television and on the movie screen. How true are the scenes depicted? Do the bad guys always fall immediately to the ground after being shot? How vulnerable is the human body? How much abuse can it take? What kills and what maims? We had the following discussion with a leading medical expert on violent deaths.

"Doctor, there are many things Hollywood has lead us to believe regarding death and dying. I wonder if you could give me the truth about them?"

"Be very happy to--ask away."

"We see a person immediately drop as soon as he has been hit by a bullet. Is this always the case and why does it happen?"

"The impact from a bullet will spin the average person around and knock him off his feet. A clean shot in the heart will drop him in his tracks. The power of a weapon stuns the body. A military bullet can lead to a cardiac arrest or convulsions."

"We see the victim's friend give him a shot of whiskey and digs a bullet out of his chest with a heated knife. Is this true to life?"

"The chest area and the abdomen are very vital areas. Usually a bullet in either of these locations will prove fatal. A bullet in the chest area may pass through the ribs and puncture a lung--collapsing it. Instead of a sling on the arm it would more likely be a tube in the chest. The patient would have considerable trouble breathing."

"In what areas particularly would a shot prove fatal?"

"As I mentioned, the heart would cause instant death. A bullet in the liver, spleen or aorta usually proves fatal because of the loss of blood."

"What happens when a large animal such as a deer is shot with an arrow versus a gun?"

"An arrow will cause the deer to bleed to death. A high velocity missle from a rifle when striking a fluid filled body acts with hydraulic force throughout the body. This force being transmitted to all parts knocks the animal off its feet. It may die from cardiac arrest or bleed to death in place."

"What happens if a person were shot in the spine?"

"A shot in the spine would cause convulsions. An acute severance of the spine will kill because of the shock to the nervous system."

"We see the Green Berets instantly kill their enemy in the movies. What do they do?"

"This should probably be called 'silent kill' rather than 'instant kill' as it is more descriptive. In the neck there are three important conduits--the spinal cord, the windpipe or trachea, and the esophagus. He slips quietly up behind his enemy, places one hand over his mouth and with his sharp stiletto thrusts it into his neck from the side--in front of the spine. With one quick motion he cuts forward severing his windpipe, the esophagus, and carotid artery. The unlucky foe is left to bleed to death."

"Is that the only way?"

"No. Another entrance point would be down through the neck area and into the lungs. In any of these quick killings, however, there will be a short quick gasp."

"Doctor, I want to thank you for your time and explanations."

"We have been talking about violent deaths. I believe you should emphasize that most deaths are peaceful. One or two last breaths and the patient passes on."

"Yes, I was with both of my parents when they died. It was as you say. They passed peacefully and quietly. May we all go that way, eh?"

"Yes, let's hope so."

14

THE BURNING QUESTION

Some planks I tore from the cabin floor, and I
lit the boiler fire;
Some coal I found that was lying around, and I
heaped the fuel higher;
The flames just soared, and the furnace roared
--such a blaze you seldom see;
And I burrowed a hole in the glowing coal, and
I stuffed in Sam McGee.

The Cremation of Sam McGee by Robert W. Service

14

Cremation is the process of destroying a body by fire and intense heat. It may be as old as man himself. The early Vikings were placed in boats, set fire and pushed out to sea. The river Ganges was the resting place for the ashes of many people from India. Until the British Government put a stop to it, many wives threw their own body on the funeral pyres of their husbands. The modern process of cremation was experimented with in England in the 1870's. It was not until 1884 that the court declared it to be legal.

Over the years it has had many advocates including George Bernard Shaw who feared that the dead would crowd the living off the earth if all bodies were preserved for the resurrection on the Judgment Day.

In answer to the strong objections from the clergy who thought it would interfere with the resurrection of the body, another advocate Lord Shaftesbury said, "What would in such case become of the Blessed Martyrs?"

Prior to the 1960's blacks were not allowed to be cremated in the south. Just as they were not allowed to use the white man's facilities in life, so also were they refused it in death.

It is a good idea for a person to check his religious tenets as some faiths strongly oppose cremation while others are neutral or encourage it.

The Roman Catholics, for instance, resist the widespread use of it. In the Jewish religion, the Orthodox regard it as unlawful, the Reformed allow it and the Conservative resist it.

Very few Protestant churches oppose it per se. A few do disapprove, but it is not absolutely forbidden. The majority accept the parishioners' choice.

Cremation is to the undertaker what "rent with the option to buy" is to the real estate broker. It defeats the purpose of the professional to make a living at his trade. A body may be delivered directly to the crematorium from the hospital without being embalmed, thus by-passing the services of a mortician. Usually, however, it is delivered by the local undertaker for which a fee is charged.

The body may be delivered to the crematorium in a bag or a fiberboard container which is burned along with the body. The cremation receptacle or "creceptacle" may also be made from other combustible materials such as wood or heavy cardboard. The container should be paint and varnish-free.

Crematoriums will not allow metal containers as this tends to "bake" the body before it cremates it.

There are certain laws regarding cremation that apply in most states. For instance, no burial or cremation can take place without a death certificate, signed by a licensed physician, stating the cause of death. Likewise, a permit is required for transit for burial in all states, but not all require a special permit for cremation.

With more and more government interference in our lives, it is interesting to note that it even carries over after death. In almost every state, a person's desire to be cremated is decided by the deceased next of kin, executor or legal custodian. This in spite of a written or verbal request prior to death.

Why would a person want his bodily remains destroyed by fire? Probably the foremost reason is that it costs less than burial in the ground with its accompanying trappings of casket, burial vault, tombstone, etc. With more religions being tolerant, and some even encouraging it, cremation has come of age.

It is clean and efficient; it can be done the day of death. These reasons plus the growing shortage of cemetery space in and around metropolitan areas have made it more popular.

Depending on the preference of the loved ones, there may be a pre-cremation memorial or service. Many prefer to have the "deed done" first and then hold the memorial service.

A pre-cremation service may be held in the crematorium chapel followed by committal of the body and cremation.

In other cases, the body is embalmed, viewed and then taken for cremation. Or the body may be viewed at the crematorium.

Still others prefer private cremation followed by a memorial service. This procedure does not allow for the committal service which is eliminated.

Some crematories have chapels available to conduct services after watching the body being "committed to the fire." Some prefer direct cremation without embalming, viewing or funeral pomp. In such cases, the undertaker transports the body from the place of death to the crematorium. Perhaps the survivors may wish a memorial service at a later date.

Crematoriums usually contain several rooms including a waiting room, chapel, committal chamber, cremation chamber, office, columbarium and urn selection room.

After the committal service and possibly in plain view of the survivors, the catafalque, on which the contained body is resting, is lowered through the floor to the committal chamber. In some crematoriums it may be taken through a door way to the committal chamber, adjacent to the cremation furnaces. Occasionally the family views the final disposition of the body into the flames.

The furnace or retort is a size in which an adult may be inserted. The furnace, generally powered by natural or bottled gas, is started.

The intense flame begins to rapidly oxidize the body tissue. This is not unlike the slower oxidation of decomposition when interred in the earth.

After the oxidation process and the water has been totally evaporated, the carbon containing portions of the body (flesh, skin, muscle, etc.) are incinerated. All that is left is the inorganic portion of the body which is the bone structure.

Approximately one and one-half hours are required for this process. In the end, an average 160 pound individual for instance, will have been reduced to five to seven pounds of ashes and bone fragments.

In England it is common to mechanically pulverize the fragments into fine powder; this is not often done in the United States although some cremations will reduce the bone fragments to a pebble-like consistency.

It is incumbent upon the crematory management to properly identify the ashes. This is accomplished by placing a numbered metallic disc in the cremation chamber with the casket.

The choice of disposal of the "ashes" is left to the next of kin. This term is not readily used by the crematory operators since it is not entirely ashes. There are fragments of bone as well. They prefer to use the term "cremains."

If the survivors are not present, or if they have not requested the undertaker to pick up the cremains, the crematory operator may, at their request, mail the cremains by parcel post to their home. This would probably be done by packing the remains in a metal box surrounded by a cardboard container. This would ensure that the ashes would not be inadvertently scattered by a careless post office worker.

The survivor may choose to purchase an urn and install the remains in a niche in a columbarium and display them with a suitable plaque, or facing plate of glass.

Some survivors proudly display their loved one's remains in an urn on their fireplace mantel. Others prefer to have them buried in a cemetery in a traditional burial setting.

The more romantic individual, the lover of nature, may request to have his remains scattered to the four winds so that they may float gently to earth in a peaceful country scene.

Practically every state will allow the scattering of the ashes on land and over water. Usually the local health deparment must be contacted as a permit may be necessary.

If burial in a cemetery is decided upon, the survivors may request an urn burial. Often a separate section of the cemetery is set aside for this. Some cemetery regulations call for a vault-like container. This may replace the urn.

Urns come in various shapes and sizes based on the survivors' preference--and the amount of remains. There are urns designed to hold the ashes of both husband and wife.

A horizontal urn is about 6-5/8" high, 8¼" wide and approximately 4" deep. It might be made from wood, bronze or marble.

Cremation is becoming more and more popular and is certainly worth considering. Those who are against it feel that there is no "body" they can visualize when tending the grave or niche. It is instead only a pile of ashes!

15

A WAKE IS AWAKE

I guide my life as I do my diet:
It's nuts to knock it before you try it.

Victor Buono

15

We are born, baptized and raised in the religious beliefs of our parents. We are eulogized according to the sectarian tenets of our church. Each faith has its own ritual and form. Whether it is the baptism, marriage or funeral ceremony, there is a church prescribed procedure.

PROTESTANT

The services are held in the funeral home, the church or occasionally the family residence. The minister conducts the service according to the traditions of its followers. A typical service is twenty minutes and consists of organ music (usually recorded if in a funeral home), prayers, sometimes a vocal solo of the deceased favorite hymn or song, poetry selections and a personal or general eulogy.

Many survivors prefer the personal eulogy, feeling that a general eulogy leaves a hollow feeling as if something were missing. The congregation is usually more touched by personal comments and thus appreciate the service more.

Funerals are becoming more a contemporary expression of the peer group. Just as a funeral service in New Orleans might consist of playing jazz, so might an alternative to a youth's service consist of pop music played by the friends of the deceased.

ROMAN CATHOLIC

The Roman Catholic funeral begins at the funeral home and proceeds to the church. The casket is brought down the aisle by the white-robed clergy. The white pall covering the casket symbolizes the white robe of baptism; the white vestments symbolize the joy of faith overcoming sadness of death. There follows a litany of prayer, liturgy of the Eucharist and communion.

JEWISH

A Jewish funeral consists of the recitation of prayers by the Rabbi expressing the spirit of Judaism and the memory of the deceased. The faith of the members in the justice of the Divine Shephard is expressed by the Twenty-third Psalm. Personal prayers and the eulogy is usually included in the service.

WAKES

The period of waiting prior to the funeral itself has generally been considered the wake. This might be held in the family home if the body is "in state" in the home. Most generally, however, the friends of the family visit the grieved ones at the funeral home during certain hours.

With the casket open and the body in view, condolences and other expressions of sympathy are given to the family.

Occasionally during this process, especially in the case of elderly deceased where the family relationship is more distant, laughter and light talk fills the funeral home. This may seem crude to a visitor just entering the room, but this could be excellent medicine for the bereaved.

Oftentimes a more formalized wake is conducted by the church which may include scripture readings, prayers and meditative responses. The Roman Catholic Church, for example, frequently conducts "The Rosary" the evening before the funeral service.

In recent times, and in some areas of the country,

the wake continues after the funeral. Those attending the
burial service are frequently asked to come to the family
home afterwards for a light lunch. This includes not only
various foods brought in by friends and neighbors, but
also alcoholic beverages. The post-funeral wake can often
be the "best party" a person attends all year!

16

THE LEGEND OF

KING MAUSOLUS

Why do cemetaries all have walls?
It's silly beyond a doubt;
The people outside don't want to get in
And the people inside can't get out!

Benny Hill, British Comedian

16

Americans waste energy, gasoline, good farm land and cemetery acreage. Presently burials in the ground fall within the area of 650 burial plots per acre. An acre could readily contain 2,000 to 3,000 plots. In fact in military areas where the graves are "row on row," as many as four thousand graves are contained within a single acre.

As a result, mausoleums have recently come more into public favor. Huge buildings able to hold crypts, tiered up to 10 levels or more, are being built in the more progressive cemeteries. They are also becoming more necessary near cities where available land for cemeteries is decreasing.

The name mausoleum was derived from one of the seven wonders of the ancient world. King Mausolus, idolized by his wife Artemisia, was honored upon his death in a way few men will ever be. She had erected, in the third century B.C. at Halicarnassus, a giant tomb 140 feet high with a perimeter of 411 feet. This must have been an awe-inspiring spectacle as its unparalleled grandeur has been retained in man's memory for over two thousand years.

Sometime between the 12th and the 15th century A.D. it was destroyed, probably by an earthquake. Parts of the original frieze are in the British Museum--that great collector of man's history.

It may be necessary eventually to do away with caskets and bury the dead in a shroud. This will allow the elements to recapture the decomposing corpse and return the remains to the earth. This is truly "ashes to ashes and dust to dust." A burial ground of this sort could inter remains indefinitely.

It is usually necessary to require embalming in above-the-ground crypts. Odor, body fluid seepage and staining of the crypt itself can result from a poorly embalmed body--or one with no embalming at all.

Another alternative is cremation. Some day the laws may require cremation, so the living are not forced into close quarters to make room for the dead.

The cremains are usually stored in an urn and placed in a niche in a columbarium. A front plate of bronze or glass seals the ashes inside and serves to identify the recessed loved one.

Occasionally one mate prefers cremation while the other prefers earth burial. It is not unusual for the ashes to be placed along side the mate so they may spend eternity together just as they spent life together.

There are some companies in different parts of the country, particularly on the West Coast, that will handle the total cremation and burial quickly and cheaply. One phone call generates the activity of collecting and transporting the body to a crematory, obtaining necessary documentation, cremating and disposing of the remains.

Family crypts are finding popularity as well. Here, up to four bodies may rest in a private tomb (or miniature mausoleum) which can be sealed effectively. This can prevent vandalizing the prominent and famous. There have been cases recently where bodies have been stolen and held for ransom. Strange ghouls walk this earth!

17

CHOOSE YOUR FINAL HOME

IF I SHOULD DIE TONIGHT

If I should die to-night
And you should come to my cold corpse and say,
Weeping and heartsick o'er my lifeless clay—
If I should die to-night,
And you should come in deepest grief and woe—
And say: "Here's that ten dollars that I owe,"
I might arise in my large white cravat
And say, "What's that?"

If I should die to-night
And you should come to my cold corpse and kneel,
Clasping my bier to show the grief you feel,
I say, if I should die to-night
And you should come to me, and there and then
Just even hint 'bout paying me that ten,
I might arise the while,
But I'd drop dead again.

Ben King

17

A casket is a rectangularly shaped box into which a body is placed. A coffin, on the other hand, is a shaped container which is wider in the shoulder area and tapers gradually toward the feet and head.

Caskets were originally made by the settlers as simple pine boxes. As settlements became more populated, the local carpenter or handyman constructed the containers for a fee.

Later as woodworking companies, such as furniture dealers, came into being, this service was a natural for them to capture.

Instead of making the caskets on demand, they were made ahead of time and stocked for immediate use. Oftentimes bodies were on display in a portion of the furniture store used for that purpose. It might seem discomforting to shop for a dining room table or bed and have a body lying in state nearby!

Nowadays the selection of a casket usually takes place in a room especially and psychologically designed to put the selector in a relaxed mood. There is no rushing and many times the selector is left alone to contemplate his loved one's final home.

The caskets, in various price ranges, are strategically placed so that selection can be made by comparison. Usually there is a larger selection of mid-price caskets from which to choose.

The lighting, the setting and the thick carpeting gives the survivors a casual ambiance in which to select the model and style. They may wander among them, touching the soft linings, rapping their knuckles against the solid exteriors and fingering the handles and latches.

There are two principle categories of design—the full couch and the half-couch. As the name implies, the full body may be viewed in the full couch. Only the top half of the body is viewed in the half-couch. Contrary to the belief of many, the body is fully clothed in both instances. The lid may be hinged in the rear or latched so the entire top lid may be removed.

A wide range of materials are used in the construction of caskets. As many as eighteen different species and grades of wood are used. The most common are pine, cedar, chestnut, elm, cherry, maple, oak, birch, cypress and maple. The finish and quality is reflected in the end price.

With reference to metals, bronze, copper and steel are the most popular. Usually the gauge or thickness is about the same as automobile fenders—and as easily dented.

In some areas, overnight service is available for casket delivery. Thus casket selection may take place from a catalog while sipping a cup of coffee and sitting in a comfortable chair.

Caskets may be selected from such names and styles as Colonial, French Provincial, Valley Forge, Monaco, Brocatelle and other glamorous names.

After the funeral and before burial, a vault encloses the casket. This is not required by law, but may be required by cemetery regulations. Their claim is that it is necessary to keep the ground from collapsing as the casket rots away.

As may be assumed, vaults are made from pretty solid material. Concrete and steel are popular with fiberglass near the top of the preference list.

There is also available in some areas, a combination casket and vault. The final closing of the body within its container takes place at the burial site, rather than at the funeral home or church, which is customary.

A concrete burial vault usually weighs over 2000 pounds. This can make it difficult to handle, transport and install. It does, however, keep the ground above it firm for a good long time.

It has only been in the last 200 years or so that all people, other than the very rich, were buried in caskets. As a result of some very scary stories of post-burial casket openings wherein the occupant was found to have moved, some complicated coffins were designed. They allowed the occupant to send a signal that he was "alive and well and living" in this enclosed box. This was accomplished through a series of pulleys, strings and bells. It is not known if any lives were saved by these ingenious designs, but it undoubtedly gave comfort to the survivors, knowing that the "state of suspended animation" was no longer to be feared.

18

CAN YOU DIG THIS?

The odds are fairly even
When your life has just begun;
But in the end, my dear old friend,
We lay you six-to-one.

Digger O'Dell, The Friendly Undertaker
(From the William Bendix Radio Show)

18

A behind the scenes look at the field of internment indicates as much specialization as industry possesses. Many cemeteries are mechanized while thousands of smaller ones still resort to manual labor--the back-breaking kind.

Opening and closing with an automatic grave-digging machine may take one-half hour. Hand labor by two good strong backs can be done in approximately $1\frac{1}{2}$ hours.

Grave holes are dug about $4\frac{1}{2}$ to 5 feet deep, 4 feet wide and 8 feet long. The spot in the cemetery where the grave is to be located is found, in many cemeteries, by small numbered cement markers just below the ground level. They designate certain areas. String lines, from marker to marker, box in an area where the grave is to be dug.

As the hole reaches a foot in depth, boards are placed around the perimeter to prevent collapsing. Progressively as the hole deepens, additional boards are added at the top, pushing down the existing ones to a lower spot. Soon the hole has reached the required depth with boards holding the sides completely except for the top one foot or so.

If a vault is to be used to surround the casket, planks are placed over the opening and the vault rolled into position. A tripod or gantry is erected and lifts the vault off the boards and rollers. The planks are removed and the vault lowered into place ready to accept the casket.

As you travel the back roads of America, a great many country churches will have, adjacent to it, a cemetery. Originally they were maintained by the church sexton. Soon the job became too large. As a result many have fallen into disrepair.

Eventually municipalities, privately-owned and operated companies, and church denominations became the major cemetery custodians.

In the older cemeteries there can be found erect head stones. Because of the cost of moving and hand trimming, many of the newer cemeteries will not allow a head stone above ground level. Thus a lawn mower easily keeps the plot and cemetery grounds trim and neat.

A backhoe is used in a great many cemeteries for opening and closing the grave. The disadvantage, of course, is the tearing up of the lawn around it. Also occasionally space to operate it presents a problem. In these cases, the only alternative is to resort to muscle power.

Two men, using back power, can refill a hole in about 45 minutes. The process is slowed down as every so often it is necessary to stop and pound the dirt down to insure there will be no sink holes later.

When removing the sod before digging the grave, squares about 4 inches deep are removed for later re-planting. As the hole is dug, twelve to fourteen wheelbarrows full of dirt are disposed of and no longer need. The amount depends upon the size of the vault which it replaces. The rest is shovelled into a pile which is covered with an artificial grass blanket during the actual service.

After the hole is dug, the vault lowered into place and the dirt covered, a "placer" is moved over the hole. This is a chrome-plated bier upon which the casket is placed by the pallbearers. Two heavy canvas straps lower the casket into the vault by slowly unwinding. Once the casket is at the bottom, the straps are slid off the ends and wound back up onto the placer. Occasionally the straps "hang up" under the casket and it is necessary to rock and jiggle the casket around to slip them loose. If someone were to open the casket later, he might think the body had been buried alive--as it might end up in a grotesque position due to this "jiggling."

Funerals are usually timed to fall during the working day of the participants. This includes, as well, the grave diggers. Since it is unwise to leave a casket unattended in a cemetery over night, the services at grave side are usually completed at least 45 minutes before quitting time at 5:00 PM. This allows the workers time to cover the grave and re-plant the sod before nightfall. Consequently those stories about drunks wandering through the cemeteries at night and falling into open graves containing caskets just don't happen—unless, of course, the gravediggers themselves were drunk and passed out. Graves dug during the day before a funeral are usually covered with boards to prevent just such accidents.

After the service and the departure of the guests, the grave diggers re-assemble. Under the watchful eye of the undertaker or his assistant, the casket is lowered into the waiting vault. The vault lid is placed over the lowered casket and sealed.

The dirt is shovelled in, tamped down and the sod is replaced. All is quiet once more in the peaceful cemetery.

19

WE TAKE IT FOR GRANITE

DUST

My desk was thick was dust, and so
My name upon it
I wrote; then with a heart aglow
Composed a sonnet.

But soon my old housekeeper came
With busy duster,
And wiping from the desk my name,
Restored it's lustre.

And then that grim Charwoman Time,
Ere Fame I tasted,
Effaced my wistful snatch of rhyme,
And it was wasted.

Ah me! The rapture, the delight,
The hope of glory!
...Our silly names in dust we write--
Dust ends the story.

Robert Service

19

Deep in the heart of the earth is a liquid core composed of nickel-iron. For millions of years it has exerted an outward pressure against the shrinking crust. This has compacted and crystallized the outer layer into enduring granite. Much of it is far below this veneer. In some areas, however, it has been exposed to the surface through the relentless erosion during the ice ages. This glacial action moving southward scraped the outer layer away and further compressed the granite under millions of tons of ice.

Of indescribable beauty and color, this granite is mined for final memorials to the dead. Removing it from the ground is a story in itself.

Using drills, some as long as 20 feet, holes are drilled one inch apart downward through the granite. The core between the holes is removed by broaching or secondary drilling. Horizontal holes are also drilled giving the rough granite block a fluted appearance when removed.

An alternate method is call "jet piercing." In this process, a high velocity flame created by burning fuel oil and oxygen is directed at the granite. By continuous flaking action the granite is removed. The flame nozzle is moved up and down making a channel two inches wide and thirty or more feet deep.

The granite is then broken into workable sizes by wedging. The wedges are forced into the previously drilled holes thus separating the block from the earth. Huge hoists lift these 35 ton monsters to the quarry's rim where they are loaded on a flat car and taken to the factory.

There the giant blocks are sawed into slabs of desired thickness. High speed circular blades with steel teeth roar through the solid granite. Carborundum and water aids the cutting process.

Another method uses a cable of fine steel drawn continously across the granite. With power applied on the flexible wire, curves and angular surfaces can be cut.

The slabs are then placed under a series of spinning "wheels," first with abrasive action, then with buffing and polishing action. This brings out the superb coloring and gives it a brilliant, mirror-like finish which neither moisture, dirt nor age can diminish.

Although power tools have replaced hand tools to a great extent, the craftsmanship in stone is still created by fine artisans. This craft is centuries old and the skillful men are proud of its traditions.

The customary hand-chisel is still used in many carvings, but for the most part they are done by a sand-blast method. A design, including letters, is first cut into a rubbery stencil which is placed over the stone. A jet-like stream of sand is shot through a nozzle into the stencil, cutting the design deeply and cleanly into the granite. The expert handwork follows as flowers and other designs are shaped.

Depending upon the belief of the deceased, designs can be carved into the final monument indicating his or her religion. As an example, a Star or Shield of David might be carved into the headstone of a Hebrew male; whereas the Menorah or candelabra would signify the final resting place of his wife.

A beautiful bronze casting with names and dates may be mounted on a granite foundation of harmonizing colors. This enhances the beauty of the flat marker as well as performing a lasting function. Various designs cast in the bronze include roses, dogwood, pine needles, ivy and oak leaves.

Personal mausoleums may be selected to contain up to a family of four or for a single casket only. They are crafted from flawless granite, factory assembled into unitized structures and are delivered as one complete unit. Thus there is no on-site construction or erection technicalities. Various designs include two over and two under, one over and one under, two horizontal and three vertically. The weight varies from 9,000 to 18,000 pounds.

Tombstones are once more becoming more personalized. If one wanders through an old, old cemetery, he will often see touching and extremely personal poems and carvings made in a long ago time. In more recent times, the memorials have been more standard designs with such epitaphs as "Sleep Peacefully," "Onward to The Glory," "The world is now a better place because he walked this way," and "A stranger to no one--a friend to all."

Now, however, tombstones are customized to tell more about the deceased than "born and died." A picture can be carved into the granite marker in three lifelike shades.

Various scenes may be depicted such as a sailing, hunting or fishing panorama. Mountain sunsets, children's drawings and picture of a favorite pet can be included on the memorial.

Touching monuments such as a young boy's childish scrawl under a drawing of his favorite toy permanently captures a moment of time that parents will long cherish.

As in ages past when the mighty Pharoahs had scenes of their life carved into stone for eternity, so now can we immortalize the lives of our loved ones.

GLOSSARY

AUTOPSY: A post-mortem examination of a body to discover the cause of death.

BLANKET: Collection of fresh flowers attached to burlap bagging and placed over the casket.

CADAVER: A dead body used for dissection--usually for medical purposes.

CASKET: Rectangular shaped container to hold the dead.

CATAFALQUE: A temporary frame used to support the casket during an elaborate funeral.

COFFIN: Burial receptacle which tapers toward the head and foot and widens at the shoulders.

COLONADE (Mausoleum): Two, four or more columns topped with a capstone.

COLUMBARIUM: Buildings with niches for placement of cremation urns.

CORONER: Elected official whose duty is to determine the cause of death when it is not apparently due to natural causes.

CORPSE: A dead body.

CRECEPTACLE: The container into which the cremated remains of an individual are placed. See also urn.

CREMAINS: The cremated remains of a human being.

CREMATION: The process of reducing a dead body to ashes by intense heat.

CREMATORIUM: A building containing the furnace or retort used to perform cremation.

CRYPT: A burial chamber within a mausoleum.

DEATH:
- **APPARENT:** A period during which manifestations of life such as body warmth, heart action and breathing is feebly maintained.

- **BIOLOGIC:** When many specialized cells have died. The others have changed beyond redemption and restoration to life is impossible.

- **CELLULAR:** The point at which all cells have ceased to function.

- **CLINICAL:** The cessation of cardiac and respiratory activity.

- **LEGAL:** Same as clinical death; capable of being restored to life.

- **SOMATIC:** The final death; death of the entire organism.

DEATH RATTLE: A gurgling sound from the dying created by lung deflation through mucous-filled passages.

DEATH STRUGGLE: The heroic attempts of a dying body to sustain life; often expressed in muscular twitching and semi-convulsions.

DEATH TRANCE: A period which may last several days during which most signs of death, such as muscle rigidity, feeble pulse and respiration and lower body temperature are present.

DEATH WEIGHT: A coin or other weight placed on the eyelids to keep them closed after death.

EMBALMER: A person licensed by the state to embalm the dead.

ENTOMBMENT: The placing of a casket in a crypt above ground.

EXEDRA: An alcove with bench attached where one goes to meditate about the dead.

EXHUME: To dig up a previously buried casket.

FLAT MARKER: A cemetery marker lying flush with the ground to permit easy lawn care.

FUNERAL: The ceremony of recognizing the dead and accompanying the remains to its final resting place.

FUNERAL DIRECTOR: A person licensed by the state to oversee the disposition of the body and be responsible for funeral protocol.

FUNERAL CHAPEL: Place devoted to preparing the dead for burial.

FUNERAL HOME: See Funeral Chapel.

GRAVE: An opening in the ground into which is placed the dead.

GRAVE LINERS: Sectional boxes into which is placed the casket.

INTERNMENT: Burial of the deceased in the ground.

INURNMENT: Placing of the burial urn in a niche.

MAUSOLEUM: Above ground structures to entomb the dead.

MEDICAL EXAMINER: Appointed official who is a physician and usually a trained pathologist and whose duty is to determine cause of death when it is not apparently due to natural causes.

MEMORIAL HOME: See Funeral Chapel.

MONUMENTS: A memorial constructed to remember the deceased.

MORTICIAN: See Embalmer and Funeral Director.

MORTUARY: See Funeral Chapel.

NECROBIOSIS: Death and replacement of cells during normal activity.

NECROPHILE: A person with an erotic fascination of, and attraction to, the dead.

NECROSIS: Death of a group of cells in a localized area.

PALL: A covering, usually made of velvet, for a casket, hearse or tomb.

SARCOPHAGUS: An elaborate above ground crypt, usually inscribed.

SHROUD: A cloth used to wrap a corpse for burial.

SPRAY: An arrangement of flowers made from burlap bagging placed over the foot of a casket.

SUSPENDED ANIMATION: A period during which breathing has ceased and other signs of apparent death are manifested.

UNDERTAKER: See Embalmer and Funeral Director.

UNDERTAKING ESTABLISHMENT: See Funeral Chapel.

URN: A container for cremated remains.

VAULT: Enclosure in which the casket is place.

BIBLIOGRAPHY

Budge, E. A., **The Book of the Dead**, New York: Bell Publishing Co., Division of Crown Publishers, Inc. by arrangement with University Books, Inc. Copyright MCMLX

Callaway, C. F., **Text Book of Mortuary Practice**, Chicago: Undertakers Supply Company, 1943

Carter, Charles F., B.S., M.D., **Microbiology and Pathology**, St. Louis: The C. V. Mosby Company, 1944

Editors, Consumer Reports, **Funerals--Consumers Last Rights** Mt. Vernon: Consumers Union, 1977

Grollman, Earl. A., **Concerning Death: A Practical Guide for the Living**, Boston: Beacon Press, 1974 (Under the Auspices of: Unitarian Universalist Association).

Habenstein, Robert W. and Lauers, William M., **Funeral Customs the World Over**, Milwaukee: Bulfin Printers, Inc. 1960

Irion, Paul., **Cremation**, Philadelphia: Fortress Press, 1968, Second Printing, 1976

Irion, Paul., **The Funeral: Vestige or Value**, Nashville: Parthenon Printing, 1966

Karsner, Howard T., M.D., **Human Pathology**, Sixth Edition, Philadelphia, Montreal, London: J. B. Lippincott Co., 1942, Reprinted 1945

Kubler-Ross, Elisabeth, **Death: The Final Stage of Growth**, Englewood Cliffs, N. J.: Prentice-Halls Inc., 1975

Langone, John, **Vital Signs**, Boston-Toronto: Little, Brown and Company, 1974

Martin, Edward A., B.A., **Psychology of Funeral Service**, Grand Junction: Sentinel Printers, 1947

N. F. D. A., **The Funeral From Ancient Egypt to Present Day America**, Milwaukee: N. F. D. A., 1916

Pine, Vanderlyn R., **Caretaker of the Dead**, New York: Irvington Publishers, Inc., 1975

Strub, Clarence G., L.E., and Frederick, L. G., "Darko," L. E.-L.F.D. **The Principles and Practice of Embalming**, Dallas: Lawrence G. "Darko" Frederick, Co-Author Owner and Publisher, 4th Edition, 1970

Turner, Ann Warner, **House for the Dead**, New York: David McKay Company, Inc., 1976

EPILOGUE

I have no doubt at all the Devil grins,
As Seas of ink I splatter.
Ye gods, forgive my "literary" sins--
The other kind don't matter.

Robert W. Service